NATIONAL GEOGRAPHIC

School Publishing

Places in My Community

Zeina Mahran

PICTURE CREDITS

Illustration by Roberto Fino (4–5).

Cover, 9 (above), 12, 16 (center left), Bill Aron/PhotoEdit, Inc.; 1, 4 (all), 5 (left), 7 (all), 8 (all), 11 (left), 14 (below left & above left), 16 (above right, center right, below left & below right), Photolibrary.com; 2, 6, 11 (above), 16 (above left), APL/Corbis; 5 (right), 11 (below right), Michael Newman/PhotoEdit, Inc.; 9 (below), 10, 13 (below left), 14 (right), Getty Images; 13 (above right), Mary Kate Denny/PhotoEdit, Inc.; 15 (above), Steve Skjold/PhotoEdit, Inc.; 15 (below) Jeff Greenburg/PhotoEdit, Inc.

Produced through the worldwide resources of the National Geographic Society, John M. Fahey, Jr., President and Chief Executive Officer; Gilbert M. Grosvenor, Chairman of the Board; Nina D. Hoffman, Executive Vice President and President, Books and Education Publishing Group.

PREPARED BY NATIONAL GEOGRAPHIC SCHOOL PUBLISHING

Ericka Markman, Senior Vice President and President Children's Books and Education Publishing Group; Steve Mico, Senior Vice President and Publisher; Marianne Hiland, Editorial Director; Lynnette Brent, Executive Editor; Michael Murphy and Barbara Wood, Senior Editors; Bea Jackson, Design Director; David Dumo, Art Director; Margaret Sidlowsky, Illustrations Director; Matt Wascavage, Manager of Publishing Services; Sean Philpotts, Production Manager.

MANUFACTURING AND QUALITY MANAGEMENT

Christopher A. Liedel, Chief Financial Officer; Phillip L. Schlosser, Director; Clifton M. Brown III, Manager.

BOOK DEVELOPMENT

Ibis for Kids Australia Pty Limited.

Published by the National Geographic Society
1145 17th Street, N.W.
Washington, D.C. 20036-4688

ISBN: 0-7922-6053-8

Fifth Printing June 2018
Printed in the United States of America

Contents

Places to Live

A community has places
where people live.

apartments

town houses

neighborhood

6

houses

mobile homes

Places to Work

A community has places where people work.

fire station

restaurant

Places to Shop

A community has places where people shop.

grocery store

shoe store

Places to Learn

A community has places where people learn.

museum

school

Places to Play

A community has places where people play.

basketball court

playground

Places to Do Things Together

A community has places
where people do things together!

community garden

neighborhood art project

swimming pool

community festival

13

14

A community has many different kinds of places. What places are in your community?

community

house

live

park

play

school

shop

store

15

Picture Glossary

house

library

playground

school

store